P9-DWD-023

WITHDRAWN

PALOS VERDES LIBRARY DISTRICT

DATE DUE

NOV 2 5 1997

MAR - 9 1998

MAR 3 1 1998

JAN 1 9 1999

NOV - 2 2000

AUG 0 7 2001

DEC 9 2001

MAR 1 1 2002

MAR 1 1 2002

MAR 1 9 1997

Palos Verdes Library District

DOROTHY HAMILL

by
William R. Sanford
&
Carl R. Green

New York

Maxwell Macmillan Canada
Toronto

Maxwell Macmillan International
New York Oxford Singapore Sydney

Library of Congress Cataloging-in-Publication Data
Sanford, William R. (William Reynolds), 1927–
    Dorothy Hamill / by William R. Sanford and Carl R. Green. — 1st ed.
        p. cm. — (Sports immortals)
    Includes index.
    Summary: A biography of the 1976 Olympic gold medalist in figure skating who originated a maneuver known as the
"Hamill camel."
    ISBN 0-89686-779-X
    1. Hamill, Dorothy, 1956–   —Juvenile literature. 2. Skaters—United States—Biography—Juvenile literature.
[1. Hamill, Dorothy, 1956– . 2. Ice skaters.] I. Green, Carl R. II. Title. III. Series.
GV850.H3S26   1993
796.91'092—dc20
[B]   92-21356

Photo Credits
All photos courtesy of AP—Wide World Photos.

Copyright © 1993 by Crestwood House, Macmillan Publishing Company

All rights reserved. No part of this book may be reproduced or transmitted in any form or by any means, electronic or
mechanical, including photocopying, recording, or by any information storage and retrieval system, without permission in
writing from the Publisher.

Macmillan Publishing Company   Maxwell Macmillan Canada, Inc.
866 Third Avenue   1200 Eglinton Avenue East
New York, NY 10022   Suite 200
                                    Don Mills, Ontario M3C 3N1

CRESTWOOD HOUSE

Macmillan Publishing Company is part of the Maxwell Communication Group of Companies.

Produced by Flying Fish Studio

Printed in the United States of America

First edition

10 9 8 7 6 5 4 3 2 1

Contents

RISKING IT ALL

Everyone's advice was the same. "Turn pro while you're ahead," her friends told Dorothy Hamill. Even her coach advised her to quit. "You have so much to lose," Carlo Fassi told her. "You are the Olympic champion. It is enough."

Fresh from her Olympic victory at Innsbruck, Austria, 19-year-old Dorothy did not agree. The 1976 World Figure Skating Championships were only three weeks away. Even though she was an ice skating superstar, she had never won the world title.

Offers from agents and producers were piling up on Dorothy's desk. If she lost her last **amateur** competition, her value as a **professional** skater would drop. But Dorothy had not reached the top by taking the safe road. She weighed the risks while she toured Vienna. Then she announced that she would skate for the world title at Göteborg, Sweden.

For two weeks Dorothy worked out every day. During practice she put everything but skating out of her mind. She ignored the talk of television specials and ice show contracts. By the time she

TRIVIA | How old was Dorothy when she first performed the Hamill camel in competition?
1*

* Answers to all Trivia Quiz questions can be found on pages 46–47.

American figure skating legend Dorothy Hamill

flew to Sweden, she felt she was ready. Her father, Chalmers Hamill, flew in to watch her skate. Her mother, Carol Hamill, stayed in her hotel room. After the stress of the Olympics, she was too tense to watch her daughter compete again.

The competition was divided into three parts. First came the **school figures**, which demanded precise, controlled skating. Next came the **short program** with its compulsory jumps and spins. Dorothy, second after the school figures, took the lead with a fine short program. That left only the **long program** with its four minutes of **free skating**.

When her music started, Dorothy moved on a tide of emotion. Her dazzling smile flashed as she glided through one difficult move after another. When she ended the program with her trademark **Hamill camel**, the crowd cheered wildly. American flags waved as she skated off the ice.

Dorothy saw her father running toward her. The joyous look on his face told her that she had won. Minutes later the band played the "Star-Spangled Banner" as Dorothy stood on the winner's platform. Tears stung her eyes.

The Olympic victory, she felt, had been for her country. The world title was for her and for all the people who had helped her. Was it only 11 years ago she had learned to skate on the pond behind Jonsie's house?

TRIVIA 2 Dorothy successfully defended her U.S. Ladies' Senior title in 1975, but only by a tiny margin. How many points separated Dorothy and runner-up Wendy Burge when the final scores were tallied?

Nineteen-year-old Dorothy Hamill performs in the free skating event of the 1976 World Figure Skating Championships in Göteborg, Sweden.

A SKATING CHILDHOOD

Dorothy was a chunky eight-year-old when she first wobbled onto the ice of Morse's Pond. The pond lay behind the Connecticut home of her grandparents, Willis and Jonsie Clough. Dorothy wore a hand-me-down pair of skates that were too large for her. Years later she said, "As I felt the ice under my blades, something inside me surged."

After that first taste of skating, the Hamills could not keep their daughter indoors. Dorothy skated on Morse's Pond until she shivered with cold, then rushed back to her grandmother's house. In the warm kitchen Jonsie rubbed the girl's feet with a warm towel. Then she gave her a cup of coffee laced with sugar and cream. Warmed inside and out, Dorothy was soon ready to skate again.

The future champion had been born in Chicago, Illinois, on July 26, 1956. Chalmers and Carol already had two children, Sandy and Marcia. Chalmers soon moved the family to Riverside, Connecticut, where he worked for Pitney Bowes. With grandparents nearby, the Hamill children grew up in a close and loving family.

Early in the winter of 1964 Dorothy fell in love—with a pair of white skates. "Wait until Christmas," Carol said. Dorothy did not give up. She begged nonstop, day after day. Finally, she came home from school one day to find a box on the kitchen table. She ripped the box open and pulled out the beautiful skates.

Marcia took her sister to nearby Morse's Pond. As Dorothy skated slowly near the edge, she saw Marcia and her friends skating backward. She tried to copy the older girls but she fell again and again. The afternoon that had started so well ended in tears.

Carol agreed that lessons might solve the problem. By her eighth lesson Dorothy had learned to reverse from a forward to a backward skating position. She was pleased to learn that the turn had a name—the mohawk. Without knowing it, she had taken her first step toward an Olympic medal.

That summer the Hamills enrolled Dorothy in classes at a nearby rink. The teacher took one look at Dorothy's beloved skates and shook her head. "Those skates don't have any ankle support," she warned. That weekend the Hamills went shopping. The skates Dorothy needed were on sale, marked down to $12.50. Jonsie talked Carol into buying them.

Dorothy's love of sports soon forced her to make a tough choice. Her friends wanted her to swim with their team on Wednesday mornings. But that was the day Dorothy took her skating lessons. Carol reminded her that the family had spent good money for skates and lessons. Now it was Dorothy's turn to stick to her commitment.

Caught up in the lessons, Dorothy forgot about the swim meets. She learned to do a counterclockwise mohawk and a bunny hop. Mastering her first jump earned her a free lesson with Barbara Taplan. Afterward Taplan told Carol that Dorothy showed real promise. "Sign her up for private lessons," she advised.

Working with Taplan proved to be a turning point. The skills Dorothy learned in the months that followed built the foundation for her later success.

THE FIRST TASTE OF COMPETITION

In the fall of 1965 Chalmers drove Dorothy to Central Park in New York City. There she entered her first competition, the Wollman Open. The nine-year-old had worked long hours to perfect her routine. By then she had mastered the bell jump and the waltz jump. In the bell jump Dorothy clapped her feet together while in the air. The waltz jump required that she make a half turn before her skates touched the ice again.

Dorothy worried that she wasn't good enough. "Just have fun," her father told her. When her turn came, her shaky nerves steadied. With Taplan's help she had learned to skate in rhythm to the beat of the music. Dorothy's spirits soared when she won second place in a field of over 100 girls.

When spring came, Dorothy began taking lessons from Otto Gold. Gold was a big bear of a man who shouted when he was upset. But he was a fine teacher of school figures. Dorothy says that school figures are to a skater what scales are to a pianist. All advanced figures are based on these simple, precise moves.

The **United States Figure Skating Association** uses a series of tests to measure a skater's skill level. Young skaters must pass a Preliminary test. After that come eight more tests. The last test qualifies skaters to enter Senior events. Dorothy joined the Southern Connecticut Figure Skating Club so that she could take her tests.

Mrs. Gold helped Carol make Dorothy's dress for the Preliminary test. Otto Gold frowned when he saw it on the day of the test. "Too long," he said. As Dorothy waited for her turn, Carol put in a new hem. Dorothy was so proud of the dress that she forgot the butterflies in her stomach. She sailed through the seven required figures without a mistake.

Dorothy's life was now centered on skating. She missed spending time with her friends, but she gladly paid the price. When the school year ended in 1966, she went to live with Coach Gold and his family in Lake Placid, New York. The arrangement allowed her to train every day. That summer she passed her first and second level tests. Each test required a higher level of control and flexibility.

After her success at the Wollman Open, Dorothy was eager to win more medals. Her technique did not match her ambition. She entered a free skating event and finished eighth. The judges were kind, she admitted later. That same week she entered a pairs competition with a friend. Gold told the girls they were not ready, but they vowed to prove him wrong. After they skated poorly, they knew that four days of practice had not been enough.

In the fall, Gold moved to Canada. Back with Barbara Taplan, Dorothy skated as a Juvenile in the North Atlantic Championships. At that point the Intermediate, Novice, Junior, and Senior levels still lay ahead. After placing sixth in school figures, Dorothy thought she performed well in the free skating. She was proud of her double salchow, which required two full turns in the air. The judges thought otherwise. Low marks in the free skating dropped her to eighth place.

Taplan talked to the Hamills. "She needs more skating time, more lessons, more concentration," she said. "It's going to be expensive."

Carol asked a single question. "Do you really believe Dorothy has the talent it takes?"

Taplan nodded. "I know she has," she said.

EARLY MORNING PRACTICES AND PIERCED EARS

From that day on, the alarm clock rang early in the Hamills' house. Dorothy and her mother rose at 5:30 to drive to the rink. Figure skaters had to take **patch time** when they could get it. Dorothy's "patch" was a section of ice reserved for her. While she skated, Carol watched from the seats beside the rink.

After warm-ups Dorothy practiced her school figures. First she would skate a circle. Then she would try to trace a second circle over the same blade marks. Soon she was dreaming about circles and figure eights. In her nightmares she looked back to see that she'd left one tiny circle inside a huge outer circle. The rink in Greenwich was too small for speed and the roof too low for jumps. Dorothy used the rest of her ice time to practice spins. She worked on camels, laybacks, sit spins and scratch spins.

Early rising meant a seven o'clock bedtime. Dorothy worried that her schoolmates would tease her if they knew. Carol agreed to tell anyone who called that Dorothy was out for the evening. Her sister Marcia knew better. She shared a room with Dorothy and the early bedtimes annoyed her. Before long the sisters were fighting over the room, their clothes and their chores.

Even though she slept in the car, Dorothy started each school day feeling tired. Her teachers were not amused when she fell asleep in class. At night she sometimes lay awake listening to the sounds of other kids playing outdoors. "It was rough at times," Dorothy said later on. "I felt bad that I could never go to my friends' slumber parties. But I never skipped a lesson."

The endless hours of practice paid off. Dorothy won her first gold medal at the Wollman Open in 1967. Later that year the great

The moves that Dorothy first learned as a child she perfected in her teenage years.

Swiss coach Gustave Lussi took her on as a student. Dorothy joined Lussi at Lake Placid and quickly earned his wrath. He took one look at her and made her spit her chewing gum into his hand. Then he smiled. "We will begin," he said.

Under Lussi's coaching, Dorothy began work on the **double axel**. The advanced jump called for her to rotate 2 ½ times after takeoff. One afternoon she fell seven times trying to complete the jump. Lussi took her aside. "You have to believe you can do it," he told her. "You have to have guts to be a great skater."

Lussi's teaching began to take hold. Dorothy passed the necessary tests and looked ahead to the end-of-summer competitions. On her 11th birthday her friends gave her 13 pairs of earrings. "Win your event," her parents wrote, "and you can have your ears pierced." A worried Dorothy wrote back asking what would happen if she came in second. "In that case you can have one ear pierced," Carol answered. "Take third and you can have your *nose* pierced," Chalmers added.

Dorothy did not have to face that problem. She won the free skating competition and earned the right to have both ears pierced. Christmas brought her another exciting present. Her parents promised to take her to the 1968 National Figure Skating Championships. "You should see the nation's best skaters perform," they told her. "Some day," they added, "you'll be competing at that level."

TRIVIA 3
Like most figure skaters, Dorothy needed two pairs of skates when she entered a figure skating competition. Why?

MOVING UP IN THE SKATING WORLD

Dorothy was turning into an ice skating vagabond. In 1968 she spent a third summer at Lake Placid, her second with Coach Lussi. Each time she mastered a new move, Lussi challenged her with a harder jump.

In the **double lutz**, a jump which was invented by Lussi, Dorothy picked up speed while skating backward. Then she lifted herself high in the air and completed two full turns before landing. When she hit the jump cleanly, she landed on one foot, still skating backward. The double flip was similar, except that she took off while skating forward.

Lussi rewarded his skaters by setting out a row of coins. The double lutz was worth two quarters, but the prize eluded Dorothy for days. At last she hit both the double lutz and the double flip on the same afternoon. Dorothy framed the hard-won coins and hung them on her bedroom wall.

The young skater passed her Fifth Test that summer. Lussi told her she was ready to compete at the Novice level. With Barbara Taplan coaching her again, she finished third in the Eastern Sectionals. Her strong showing qualified her for the Nationals in Seattle, Washington.

The Hamills believed that Taplan had taken their daughter as far as she could. Now they hired Sonya Dunfield as Dorothy's coach. The former national champion worked on the girl's old bugaboo, the school figures. As the trip to Seattle neared, Dorothy could scarcely eat. The 12-year-old admitted that she was afraid the plane would crash.

When she reached Seattle, Dorothy skated the school figures poorly. Despite her sixth place standing, though, she felt ready for the final day. Free skating was her strength. At the last minute the thought of performing in front of 10,000 people gave her stage fright. Dunfield knew what to do. She told Dorothy to forget everything but the ice. Then she gave her student a gentle push.

Early in her routine Dorothy landed the double lutz cleanly. She smiled and began to enjoy herself. Then, near the end, the crowd's applause broke the spell. She lost her balance during a double toe loop and fell. Instantly she popped up and finished as strongly as she had begun. The judges overlooked her fall. The high marks they gave her made Dorothy the National Novice champion.

The young champion passed her Seventh Test during the summer of 1969. Then she joined Coach Lussi at Lake Placid. Lussi was now offering three quarters for a perfect triple salchow. Where the double lutz had required two turns in the air, the triple salchow required three. Frequent falls bruised Dorothy's arms and legs. She sometimes limped, but she did not give up.

In November the Hamills went to Buffalo, New York, for Dorothy's first Junior competition. Disaster struck when Chalmers took his daughter to a small rink in Canada to practice. During warm-ups Dorothy skated into a rope stretched across the rink. She bounced back, fell and hit her head on the ice. A doctor looked at the lump and said she should forget the regionals.

TRIVIA 4

In 1976 Dorothy added her name to the list of women figure skaters who won the U.S. Nationals, the Olympics and the World titles in the same year. Who are her partners on this grand slam roster?

16   *Throughout the highs and lows of practice sessions and competitions, Dorothy could always count on the love and support of her parents.*

Despite her protests, the Hamills took Dorothy home for X rays. The injury healed quickly and skating officials allowed her to enter the Eastern Regionals. Skating in Boston, Massachusetts, that December, she again fell behind in the school figures. Then she roared back with an outstanding performance in the free skating. Once again Dorothy knew the joy of hearing her name announced as the gold medal winner.

THE HIGH PRICE OF EXCELLENCE

Every star athlete makes sacrifices. Figure skaters make more than most. Dorothy gave up normal bedtimes and a normal teenage life. When she did have a boyfriend, she had to sandwich dates between practice sessions. Her practice and travel schedule forced her to drop out of public school when she was 14. From then on she studied with tutors or took classes at private schools.

Dorothy's skating required equal sacrifices by her family. Carol drove her to morning practices and waited to drive her home again. On winter mornings she shivered and sipped hot coffee to keep from freezing. When Dorothy flew to competitions, Carol or Marcia went with her. Dorothy was maturing as a skater, but she was still a young girl. She needed her family close by.

As an amateur, Dorothy could not accept prize money when she skated. Unlike many foreign skaters, American skaters were

TRIVIA 5 Dorothy was only one of three figure skaters who made the U.S. women's team in 1976. Because of her success, the other two are often overlooked. Who were they?

not sponsored by the government. Lessons, rink time, equipment and clothing all ate into the family budget. Dorothy spent about $600 a year on skates. Skating costumes cost as much as $300 each. Then came bills for plane tickets, lessons, music tapes and rink fees. The list seemed endless. In some years the bills added up to more than $25,000.

Skating boots were a special expense. Because Dorothy had an extra bone in her ankle, new boots often caused blisters. Carol sometimes punched out the leather to relieve the pressure. At other times Dorothy padded her boots with foam rubber. Finally in 1969 Coach Dunfield took her to a custom boot shop in New York. There a craftsman made molds of her feet. A week later Dorothy pulled on her first pair of custom-made boots. They felt "like two blocks of concrete," she complained. Two weeks later they began to feel "pretty good." After four weeks Dorothy knew they were the best boots she had ever worn.

Along with buying custom boots, the Hamills paid for lessons with topflight coaches. After working with Taplan, Lussi and Dunfield, Dorothy met Carlo Fassi in Japan in 1971. Fassi had been Peggy Fleming's coach when she won the 1968 Olympics. Better still, he specialized in teaching the school figures. By that time Dorothy had passed her Eighth Test and was skating at the Senior level. Now she was competing against world-class skaters like Janet Lynn and Julie Holmes.

Fassi's high fees were only part of the costs for the Hamills, who had to follow him wherever he went. At first Dorothy lived with the Fassi family in Tulsa, Oklahoma. When the coach moved to Lake Placid for the summer, she went with him. Carol joined Dorothy for a later move to Denver, Colorado. In Denver their tight budget barely paid for food and a small apartment. When she wasn't practicing, Dorothy took classes at the Colorado Academy.

Little by little, Fassi smoothed out the last rough spots in Dorothy's skating. He insisted that she focus on what she was doing. That was one more sacrifice. She agreed to give up daydreaming while she practiced the boring school figures.

With the help of Carlo Fassi, Dorothy developed a strong yet graceful skating style.

THE LONG ROAD TO THE OLYMPICS

January of 1971 was a big month for Dorothy. She skated to the music of Stravinsky's *Firebird* as she prepared for the Senior Nationals. Carol made her a brilliant red dress for the big event. A butterfly pattern of beads sparkled as she spun into her jumps. Coach Lussi's words still echoed in her ears. "Such a jumper," he had said. "I never knew a girl who jumped so big."

Dorothy's shaky school figures left her far back in the field. As often happened she came back strong the next day. Her all-out free skating performance earned her an ovation and a fifth place overall. Then came a lucky break. The fourth place skater retired. U.S. officials asked Dorothy to take her place in the Pre-Olympic Championships in Sapporo, Japan.

Dorothy was amazed to see herself featured in Japanese magazines. Reporters began calling her the Little Princess. When competition started, she finished third in the figures. The friendly crowd cheered when she wore her *Firebird* dress for the free skating. Dorothy rewarded her fans with a strong performance that earned a silver medal. Julie Holmes captured the gold. A day later the American girls put on a special show for Japan's crown prince.

 TRIVIA 6 Dorothy won a gold medal at her only Olympics, but two other women hold *five* Olympic gold medals between them. Name the Norwegian who won three gold medals before World War II and the German skater who won two gold medals during the 1980s.

"The best thing about the trip to Japan," Dorothy said later, "was meeting Carlo Fassi." Fassi did more than help her skating. He also discovered that she was nearsighted. Fassi told the eye doctor, "She needs very big glasses. That way she can see out the corners to do the figures." Those oversize glasses later became one of Dorothy's fashion statements.

Later that year Dorothy won gold medals in France and Germany. Those big wins raised her hopes for skating in the 1972 Winter Olympics. The top three skaters in the 1972 Nationals would earn the right to skate for the U.S. After fighting off a bad case of the flu, Dorothy traveled to California to compete in the Nationals.

Her chances looked good when she finished fifth in the school figures. Then she turned in what she thought was a near-perfect free skating routine. The judges did not agree. Dorothy's marks left her fractions behind the third place skater. Fourth place was not good enough to make the team. The Hamills tried to cheer her up with a trip to Disneyland, but she could not stop the tears.

The top American skaters turned pro after the 1972 Olympics. During the next two years Dorothy proved she was ready to take their place. She won her first Senior National Championship in January of 1974. A month later she went to Germany for the World Championships.

Just before her free skating program Dorothy heard a chorus of boos. Certain the audience was booing her, she broke into tears. She calmed down when told that the jeers were for the judges. Back in control, Dorothy glided onto the ice and skated superbly. One judge gave her a perfect 6.0. The gutsy performance earned her a second place silver medal.

The top three finishers of the National Figure Skating Championships—Linda Fratianne (left), *Dorothy Hamill* (center) *and Wendy Burge* (right)— *represented the United States at the 1976 Winter Olympics.*

Dorothy was passing other milestones too. The Colorado Academy awarded her a high school diploma in 1975. A few months later she suffered her first serious injury. A fall during practice left her ankle badly sprained. The cast came off in time for her to take second in the 1975 World Championships. Now it was time to focus on skating's biggest event, the Winter Olympics.

COMPETING FOR OLYMPIC GOLD

Dorothy stepped up her training as the 1976 Olympics neared. She rose each day before the cold Denver dawn and skated for four hours. Then she returned to the ice in the afternoons and evenings. After skating for six days, she took ballet lessons on the seventh. Dorothy also found time for gym workouts and saunas. The workouts slimmed her 5 feet 3 inch frame to a slender 110 pounds. Twice-weekly massages eased the tension in her neck and shoulders.

Dorothy nailed down an Olympic berth by winning the Nationals for the third time. Taking first in the school figures added spice to the victory. After the Nationals she returned to Denver—and promptly lost her good spirits. Coach Fassi was busy with other skaters, leaving Dorothy feeling left out. Carol called Peter Burrows, a coach her daughter had worked with in New York. With an old friend by her side, Dorothy regained her confidence. A new and stylish haircut also helped.

Dorothy joined the U.S. team for the trip to Innsbruck, Austria. After losing the world title the year before, she was no longer rated as the favorite. Skating experts picked world champion Dianne DeLeeuw of the Netherlands to win the gold. Christine Errath of East Germany was not far behind. Despite those ratings, *Time* magazine featured Dorothy in its Olympic cover story.

 TRIVIA 7 When Dorothy joined the Ice Capades, her fellow skaters gave her a most unglamorous nickname. What did they call her?

24

Dorothy won the hearts of American skating fans with her awesome talent, unique style and cheerful disposition.

A proud Dorothy Hamill shows off her Olympic gold medal during a press conference in Innsbruck, Austria.

Butterflies danced in Dorothy's stomach as the skating began. One slip, she thought, could cost her a medal. Coach Fassi told her, "If you want to convince the judges that you are the best, you must first convince yourself." The pep talk helped. Dorothy's precise control earned her a second in the school figures. Still skating well, she took the overall lead with a strong short program. The prized gold medal now lay within reach.

The free skating finals fell on Friday, February 13. Awaiting her entry, Dorothy felt her knees trembling. She thought about the debt she owed her parents and her coaches. Then the first notes of her music focused her on the job at hand. She stroked onto the ice to a medley of themes from old Errol Flynn films.

All the years of sacrifice came down to a tense four minutes. Dorothy and her coaches knew that no one wins the Olympics with a safe program. As she wrapped herself in the "Sea Hawk" music, she glided into a series of risky jumps. Starting with a delayed axel, she added a Walley jump with a double axel, a double-toe loop and a camel spin. Then, flashing her famous smile, she soared into a double lutz, a back spiral and a double salchow. The crowd hummed as she skated and cheered when she ended with a Hamill camel. Flowers showered onto the ice as Dorothy took her bows.

Dorothy knew she had skated well. Her scores confirmed that feeling. The judges gave her 5.8s, a 5.9 and a perfect 6.0 for **technical merit**. She earned solid 5.9s for **artistic merit**. The high marks added up to 193.80 points—and the gold medal. DeLeeuw took the silver and Errath won the bronze.

The Olympic president awarded Dorothy her medal. Tears glinted in her eyes as a band played the "Star-Spangled Banner." As she said later, "I had reached the other side of the rainbow."

STARRING IN THE ICE CAPADES

After the Olympics Dorothy shook off her advisors and competed in the World Championships. When she won that title, she stood at the top of the skating world. With nothing more to prove, she felt ready to turn pro. The years of sacrifice could now be turned into cash.

Dorothy is welcomed home after her Olympic victory.

Dorothy waves to a crowd of adoring fans during a parade held in her honor. Riding alongside Dorothy in the parade float is her sister Marcia (left) *and friend Kim* (right).

The American public took Dorothy to its heart. She was young, pretty and talented. Her hometown held a parade and renamed the skating rink in her honor. Children clustered around her, begging for autographs. As she signed, Dorothy remembered an actor who had once turned his back on her. She vowed that she would never treat the public rudely.

TRIVIA 8 When Dorothy married Dean Paul Martin in 1982, she left a famous neighbor off the guest list. Who was the neighbor and why did she decide not to invite him?

Whether preparing for the Olympic Games or an Ice Capades show, Dorothy would practice her moves until her routine was as perfect as possible.

With fame came a flood of offers. After much thought Dorothy picked Jerry Weintraub to handle her business affairs. She chose him in part because he was the only agent who came to see her skate. Weintraub wanted her to perform skating shows all over the world. Dorothy said no, she preferred to skate with an ice show. In the end Weintraub hammered out a contract with the Ice Capades. The new job tied Dorothy to the show for 44 weeks each year.

Dorothy felt as though she had joined a large friendly family. The hardest part was adjusting to her new schedule. For most of her life she had risen at five and gone to bed early. Now she performed mostly at night. On many days she did not fall into bed until one or two in the morning. Two years later she was still waking up at dawn, and enjoying the luxury of going back to sleep until noon.

Now that she did not have to please judges, Dorothy skated to please her public. She drew energy from the smiling faces she saw in the audience. The applause helped her jump, spin and stroke in perfect sync with the music. Her routine lasted almost five minutes. After a break she returned to tell the crowd about her new life with the Ice Capades. Then she skated a second routine to the music of *That's Entertainment*. In her years of Senior competition Dorothy had fallen only once. Yet to her dismay she fell during her first show with the Ice Capades.

A star, Dorothy found, is always "on." Gone were the days when she could run around in jeans and a T-shirt. Her fans expected her to look good at all times. She also had to be careful of what she said, for reporters were always close by. On the road she lived out of a trunk and seldom saw her family. Interviews and photo sessions filled her time off the ice. Days off meant flying to the next city on the tour.

"I've had to fight for myself and kind of grow up overnight," Dorothy said. "It's a lot tougher than I thought it would be. 'Well,' I figured, 'it's one show every weeknight, three on Saturday, two on Sunday. Piece of cake.' Well, it's not. You're on all the time. Wherever you go, whatever you do, everybody sees you. I used to live my life and do whatever I wanted to do, but no more."

Along with her parents, Dorothy examines a portrait of herself that was displayed in New York's Madison Square Garden.

Dorothy finally takes time out for romance! She is shown here dancing with Dean Paul Martin at a popular New York disco.

BUILDING A PRIVATE LIFE

Until 1976 Dorothy was driven to excel as a skater. After her victories at Innsbruck and Göteborg, her life became more normal. Despite the demands of starring in the Ice Capades, there was time for romance.

Boyfriends had come and gone in Dorothy's life. Now, all at once, she fell in love with singer Dean Martin's son, Dean Paul Martin. The handsome actor-athlete was five years older than Dorothy. As a teenager he had hit the rock music charts as part of a trio called Dino, Desi and Billy. After playing tennis at UCLA, Dean had gone on to play semipro football and pro tennis. He had also gone through a divorce and starred in a money-losing movie. None of this bothered Dorothy. She thought he was shy, funny and sweet.

With demanding and conflicting work schedules, Dorothy and Dean spent much of their time apart. They seemed happiest during rare and brief moments together like this one.

The courtship lasted five years. Dean followed the Ice Capades around the country when he wasn't playing tennis. Summers were the hardest times. Dorothy's vacations often came when Dean was playing tennis overseas. At times the couple went months without seeing each other.

The Hamills worried about Dean's playboy past. Dorothy refused to listen to their warnings. She and Dean were married in Beverly Hills, California, on January 8, 1982. The guest list included Frank Sinatra, Kenny Rogers and Rod Stewart. Twenty-one months later, Dean moved out. "They were the all-American couple," a friend said. "It's simply a case of loving each other but not being able to live together."

Gossips said that Dorothy's sheltered life had not prepared her for a Hollywood lifestyle. Her successful career also contrasted with her husband's failure as an actor. Three years later Dean climbed into a National Guard jet for a weekend training flight. Flying in a blizzard, he crashed into a mountain and died instantly.

The bride and groom, Dorothy Hamill and Dean Paul Martin, appear before the guests attending their star-studded wedding ceremony in Beverly Hills, California.

Dorothy did not let the divorce and Dean's death slow her down. By then she had left the Ice Capades to try new skating ventures. Her public did not know the price of performing every night. At times her legs ached so badly she could not sleep. "I'm not getting any younger," she said with a smile.

To her delight she was chosen to skate in several ice ballets. Teaming with Robin Cousins, she performed the *Nutcracker* in San Francisco, California, and Seattle, Washington. Television viewers loved her ice ballet version of *Romeo and Juliet*. In 1984 she starred with John Curry's ice company. The highlight of the tour came when she skated at New York's Metropolitan Opera House. In 1985 Dorothy joined Fantasy on Ice for a 12-city tour. She also appeared in television specials with Gene Kelly, Andy Williams and Perry Como. At age 28 she was banking over $1 million a year.

New opportunities arose off the ice, too. After Carol recovered from breast cancer, Dorothy volunteered to work for the American Cancer Society. She helped raise money for research by speaking at fund-raisers. Clairol and NutraSweet hired her to endorse their products. Not to be outdone, ABC television picked her to work as a broadcaster for figure skating events.

By the time the 1990s rolled around, Dorothy's personal life was back in order. After marrying sports medicine specialist Ken Forsythe, she gave birth to baby Alexandra. When she couldn't find an ice rink near her Indian Wells, California, home, Dorothy practiced roller blading. To keep her career alive she competed in pro skating competitions and produced new ice ballets.

36   *Dorothy and ten-day-old Alexandra, each dressed in NutraSweet attire, pose for Los Angeles photographers.*

Dorothy was on hand to interview gold medal winner Kristi Yamaguchi at the 1992 Winter Olympics. At age 35, the skating immortal looked fit enough to compete for another medal.

DOROTHY HAMILL, ICE SKATING IMMORTAL

Ice skaters, like many athletes, have short careers. A young skater bursts onto the scene, wins hearts and medals and soon fades. Only a few rise to heights that carry them on to enduring fame. In ice skating, Sonja Henie is one of those figures. Dorothy Hamill is another.

March of Dimes poster child Christine Anderson gets a ride on the ice from her skating idol, Dorothy Hamill.

Figure skating immortals enjoy a golden opportunity together during an Ice Capades show. Dorothy Hamill (right), *winner of the 1976 Olympic gold medal, is shown with Peggy Fleming* (center), *the 1968 winner, and Aja Zanova* (left), *who captured the gold in 1948.*

A 1976 story in *Time* magazine described the style that made Dorothy a skating immortal. "Dorothy…performs a difficult program, works at high speed, plus she interprets the music with feeling," one of the judges said. The article went on to say that "her most beautiful move is a delayed axel in which she hangs suspended before completing $1\frac{1}{2}$ revolutions in the air. Skating fanciers also admire Dorothy's spins, high-speed yet delicate rotations within rotations. They seem effortless."

TRIVIA 9 In 1977 a magazine asked fifth graders from across the country to name their favorite athletes. The children chose Dorothy as number one on their list. Name some of the famous athletes she beat out in this survey.

Only the great skaters have jumps and spins named for them. The salchow is named for a Swedish skater, the axel for a Norwegian and the lutz for a Swiss. Dorothy invented the Hamill camel while working with Gustave Lussi. The term "camel" comes from the humped-back position skaters take when learning this spin. Dorothy's camel began with a standard flying camel layover. Then she added a new move by dropping into a sit spin with one leg extended. She used the Hamill camel for the first time in the 1970 Junior Nationals.

Dorothy receives the 1977 Women's Sport Athlete of the Year Award presented by tennis superstar Billie Jean King.

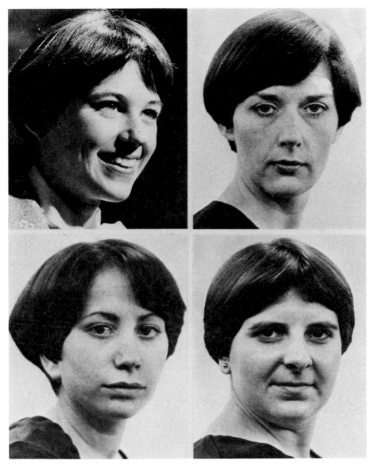

The Dorothy Hamill haircut was the hottest style among young American women after the 1976 Winter Olympics.

Many young skaters wear the popular Hamill haircut. In 1976 Dorothy despaired of finding a haircut that pleased her. A friend suggested she take her problem to Suga, a New York stylist. Suga's cut allowed her hair to stand out during a spin, then fall neatly into place. Dorothy was overjoyed. "For the first time I could remember, my hair looked good," she said.

In 1991 Dorothy received some upsetting news. The Ice Capades, the show that had meant so much to Dorothy and her career, had declared bankruptcy. Dorothy decided that "there was something there to save." With the help of her husband, Ken, and a close friend and businessman, Dorothy purchased the Ice Capades and became co-owner and president.

Looking ahead, Dorothy says, "There's so much I want to do, and I want it all now, so I keep having to tell myself it will come sooner or later. I know that, because I'm a risk taker. You don't become an Olympic champion without taking risks."

If Dorothy were skating in the Olympics today, she would not have to worry about the dreaded school figures. Why?

GLOSSARY

amateur—An athlete who competes solely for the love of sport, not for money.

artistic merit—The scores judges award a skater based on the overall beauty and grace of a free skating performance.

double axel—A figure skating jump with $2\frac{1}{2}$ turns in the air.

double lutz—A figure skating jump in which the skater takes off from the back-outside edge of one skate, rotates clockwise two times and lands on the back-outside edge of the other skate.

free skating—Any series of jumps, spins and linking movements that figure skaters perform to music.

Hamill camel—A maneuver invented by Dorothy Hamill and Coach Gustave Lussi. The Hamill camel begins with a flying camel layover and ends with a sit spin.

long program—A four-minute free skating routine that skaters create to showcase their best spins and jumps.

patch time—Practice time and space that an ice rink has reserved for a skater's use.

professional (pro)—An athlete who is paid for competing.

school figures—A series of compulsory figures that a skater must trace on the ice with great precision. Each figure is composed of two or three circles.

short program—A two-minute free skating program that includes seven required maneuvers.

technical merit—The scores judges award a skater based on the skill with which he or she performs the mechanics of skating.

United States Figure Skating Association—The organization that governs figure skating competition in the U.S.

MORE GOOD READING ABOUT DOROTHY HAMILL

Dolan, Edward F., Jr., and Richard B. Lyttle. *Dorothy Hamill: Olympic Skating Champion.* Garden City, NY: Doubleday & Co., 1979.

Fassi, Carlo. *Figure Skating with Carlo Fassi.* New York: Charles Scribner's Sons, 1980.

Hamill, Dorothy, with Elva Clairmont. *Dorothy Hamill: On and Off the Ice.* New York: Alfred A. Knopf, 1983.

Heller, Mark. *The Illustrated Encyclopedia of Ice Skating.* New York: Paddington, 1979.

Phillips, Betty Lou. *The Picture Book of Dorothy Hamill.* New York: Julian Messner, 1979.

Van Steenwyk, Elizabeth. *Dorothy Hamill: Olympic Champion.* New York: Harvey House, 1976.

DOROTHY HAMILL TRIVIA QUIZ

1: Dorothy was 13 when she added the Hamill camel to her free skating routine during the 1970 Junior Nationals. Reporters covering the competition gave the new move its catchy name.

2: Dorothy scored 183.66 points to Burge's 183.28. The winning margin was only .38 of a point.

3: Figure skaters use one pair for school figures, another pair for free skating. The first pair have short toe picks and shallow grooves along the blades to allow for precise control. The skates used for free skating have large toe picks and deep grooves which bite into the ice after a jump.

4: Dorothy was the fourth woman to win all three titles in the same year. The first three were Tenley Albright, Carol Heiss and Peggy Fleming. Kristi Yamaguchi joined that select list of skaters when she won all three titles in 1992.

5: Dorothy's teammates in 1976 were Linda Fratianne and Wendy Burge. Neither won a medal that year, but Fratianne came back in 1980 to win the silver medal. The California skater also won the U.S. Nationals four times and was world champion in 1979.

6: Norway's Sonja Henie won Olympic gold in 1928, 1932 and 1936. East Germany's Katarina Witt skated to victory in the 1984 and 1988 Winter Olympics.

7: Dorothy's friends in the Ice Capades called her Squint. The nickname was a joking reference to her poor eyesight.

8: Dorothy did not invite President Ronald Reagan to her wedding even though his California home was close by. She feared that the Secret Service guards who go everywhere with a president would disrupt the wedding.

46

9: After naming Dorothy number one, the children listed the following athletes: Nadia Comaneci (gymnastics), Bruce Jenner (decathlon), O.J. Simpson (football), Chris Evert (tennis), Lou Brock (baseball), Johnny Bench (baseball), Mark Spitz (swimming), Pete Rose (baseball) and Muhammad Ali (boxing).

10: Figure skating officials changed the nature of figure skating forever in 1990 by dropping school figures from international competition.

index